DEADLY ANTS

DEADLY ANTS

by SEYMOUR SIMON
illustrations by WILLIAM R. DOWNEY

FOUR WINDS PRESS   NEW YORK

Library of Congress Cataloging in Publication Data

Simon, Seymour.
  Deadly ants.

  Summary: Discusses some of the types of ants that can be harmful to animals
and humans, paticularly fire ants and army ants.
  1. Ants — Juvenile literature. [1. Ants] I. Downey, William. II. Title.
QL568.F7S52   595.7'96   79-14705
ISBN 0-590-07610-8

Published by Four Winds Press
A division of Scholastic Magazines, Inc., New York, N.Y.
Text copyright © 1979 by Seymour Simon
Illustrations copyright © 1979 by William R. Downey
Printed in the United States of America
Library of Congress Catalog Card Number: 79-14705

1   2   3   4   5   83   82   81   80   79

For David Reuther,
in appreciation for his help and interest,
and in friendship

You probably have ants in your home. Almost everybody has at one time or another. Ants live in forests, fields, swamps, deserts, seashores, islands, boats, airplanes, houses, farmlands, suburbs, and cities. About the only places you won't find ants are the frozen snowfields of the Arctic and Antarctic.

We don't usually think of ants as dangerous because they are so small and easily brushed aside. But some kinds of ants can be harmful to large animals and even to humans. For example, about ten thousand people each year are stung badly enough by fire ants to see a doctor. Some of the people seeking help have been painfully stung dozens and even hundreds of times.

Army ants can also be dangerous. Army ants swarm out in large raiding parties that cover the ground for hundreds of square feet. A large animal caught in their midst can be stripped right down to the bone.

This book does not tell you about all the kinds of ants that can sting or bite you. It does tell you about some of the most dangerous kinds. Mostly you will find out about two deadly ants — fire ants and army ants.

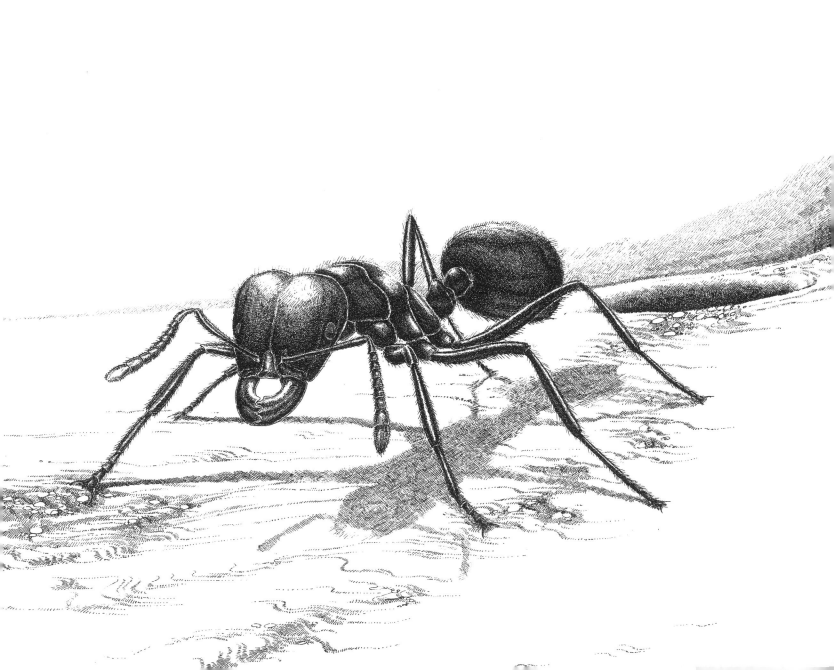

FIRE ANTS

Fire ants look like ordinary house ants that you find in your kitchen in the summer. They are about one-eighth to one-quarter inch long. Some are black, but the most dangerous kinds of fire ants are reddish-brown or dark brown in color.

Fire ants have stingers at the end of their bodies. The sting is painful and burns like fire. When disturbed, the fire ant is quick to attack both people and animals.

If one of these minimonsters crawls onto your skin to sting, you're in for trouble. The ant bites down into your skin with sharp, strong jaws. Then it bends its hind part to thrust its stinger into your flesh.

If you don't pull the fire ant away, it might swivel around and sting you several times. Afterward you can see a circle of sting marks around two central jaw bites on your skin.

A fire ant has a venom (poison) much like that of certain deadly plants. The venom acts as a nerve poison. It can instantly paralyze grasshoppers, caterpillars, earthworms, and other small animals. In larger amounts, the venom has been known to kill squirrels, pigs, chickens, and calves.

The sting feels like a fierce burning. In a few minutes, a little blister develops. This can last for a week or ten days. After the blister pops, it often leaves a small white scar which can last a lifetime.

Some people may become very ill as a result of just a few fire-ant stings. They may get dizzy, have difficulty breathing, and lose consciousness. If they are not given prompt medical treatment they may even die.

Sometimes large numbers of ants will sting a person or a large animal. Several people have died as a result of many ant stings. One young girl was stung by dozens of fire ants. She is living, but for the rest of her life she must receive monthly injections to fight the effects of the venom.

Fire ants nesting around homes, in school yards, and in parks can be dangerous to children and pets. On farms, fire-ant nests make it difficult to plow the land and plant crops. Farm workers often are badly stung while doing their chores. Sometimes workers refuse to harvest hay because fire ants make their homes in the bales and will sting anyone who comes too close.

A colony of red fire ants builds a hard-crusted nest or mound. The mound is sometimes three feet high and nearly

three feet across. The nest may go even deeper below the ground.

In some southern states, there is a mound every twenty-five feet. Fire ants build mounds in lawns, playgrounds, parks, farmlands, and grazing land.

If you split a mound down the middle, you would see a maze of tunnels and chambers. A queen ant, several thousand winged males, about a hundred female (future queen) ants, and over a hundred thousand worker ants may live in one colony.

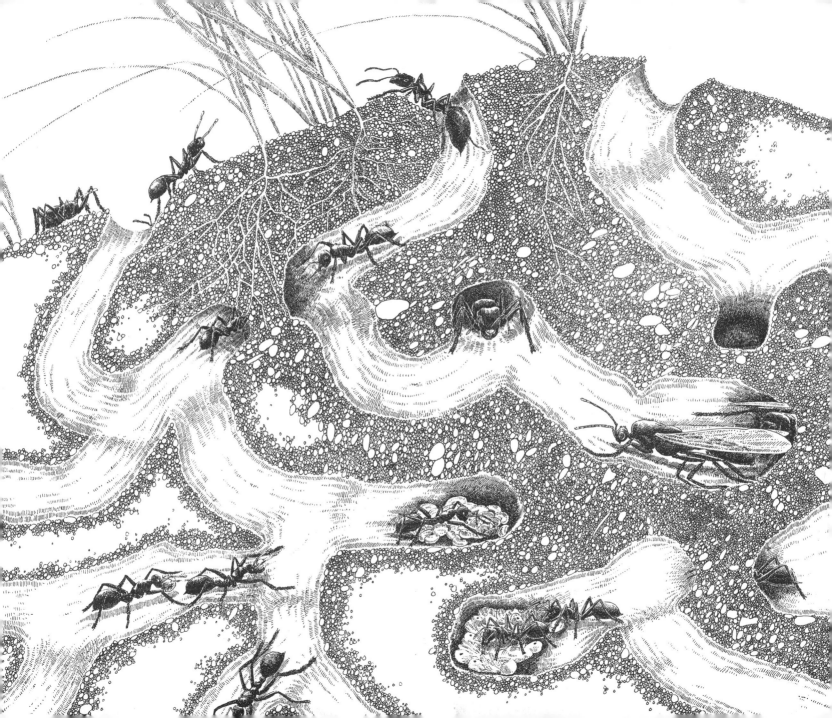

A mound protects the developing young. During hot summer weather, workers carry the eggs and cocoons to cooler underground chambers. But during cooler months, the eggs and cocoons are carried to the warmer, sunny side of the mound.

Workers guard the mound entrance. They use their feelers to check incoming and outgoing traffic. If they spot an intruder, they release a special alarm odor. The odor quickly brings forth a mass of biting and stinging ants.

On a humid day in May or June, swarms of future queens and males leave the nest on a mating flight. The new queens may be carried by winds for ten or more miles during their mating flights. But fire-ant queens landing accidentally on cars or trucks can be carried fifty or a hundred miles before they begin to nest.

After mating, each queen lands and breaks off her wings. She digs a shallow burrow in the soil and begins laying eggs to start a new colony. The male ants also land but wander aimlessly around until they die.

Black fire ants appeared in the United States in the year 1918. They had been accidentally imported from South America. They were not as pesky as the red fire ant. They could not stand harsh winter weather and they did not compete too well with native ants. The black fire ants were only a minor problem to people.

But the red fire ants were a different story. They probably came into the United States in the early 1940s. The ants were stowaways on lumber ships arriving in Alabama from the great forests of Brazil. In a short time the red fire ant lived up to its scientific name, *Solenopsis invicta*. The name means the "unconquered" ant.

The red fire ant is much fiercer than its black cousin. The black ant and other kinds of ants could not compete with the red-ant invader. After twenty years, red fire ants had covered twenty million acres of land. After just another ten years, they had spread over five times that area.

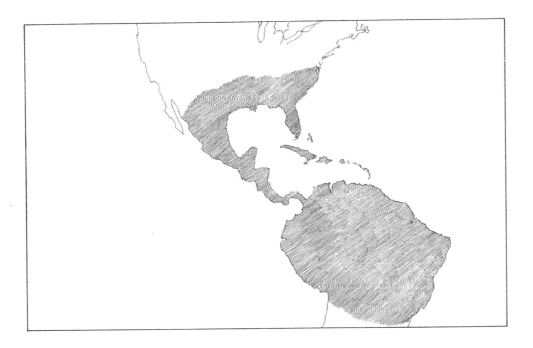

The red fire ant is found mostly in the southeastern United States, as well as in South and Central America. Over one hundred and fifty million acres in nine states are covered with fire-ant mounds.

The fire ant eats all kinds of crops as well as plants that grow wild. They also eat small animals such as insects.

Texas is probably the state most involved with stopping the fire ant. Southeast Texas has over forty million acres of land covered by fire-ant mounds. If the fire ants ever cross the rest of Texas and the deserts of the Southwest, then the large farming areas of the West Coast could be threatened.

The only real barrier against fire ants seems to be very cold weather. Red fire ants are not able to live in places where winter temperatures often go below 10° Fahrenheit (−12° Celsius). This means that fire ants could live as far north as New Jersey on the East Coast and Washington on the West Coast.

Perhaps the greatest damage from fire ants comes from the human efforts to fight them. Over one hundred million dollars have been wasted on poisonous insecticides to kill the ants. But the ant population just continues to grow larger. In the meantime, much land, wildlife, and many people have been exposed to deadly poisons.

There are many chemical sprays that will kill red fire ants. But there are very few that will kill off whole colonies of fire ants. And there are none that will kill off colonies that are also safe for people and other animals. Some of the chemicals used always wind up polluting the land and water.

Even if the chemical poisons were safe to use, they are not very good controls. The red fire ant mound itself is a good defense. The queen and the young live deep below the surface. A poison will work only if applied below ground, on the earth, and in the air at the same time. But if even one new queen escapes, a new mound will be built. So far the human war on fire ants has been a costly failure.

Some scientists are searching for other ways to fight the fire ant. They are studying the fire ants in their homeland of Brazil. They are looking for the natural enemies that help keep the red-ant population from growing too large in its homeland.

So far they have found a small mite that kills fire ants. They have also found a kind of tiny, underground ant which eats the young of the fire ant. Finally, they have found that fire ants in Brazil often are infected by a disease which leaves them weak.

In the United States, fire ants have no natural enemies. Perhaps by introducing the disease and some of their enemies, many fire ants would die of natural causes. This might keep the ant population at a low level that would not be bothersome to people.

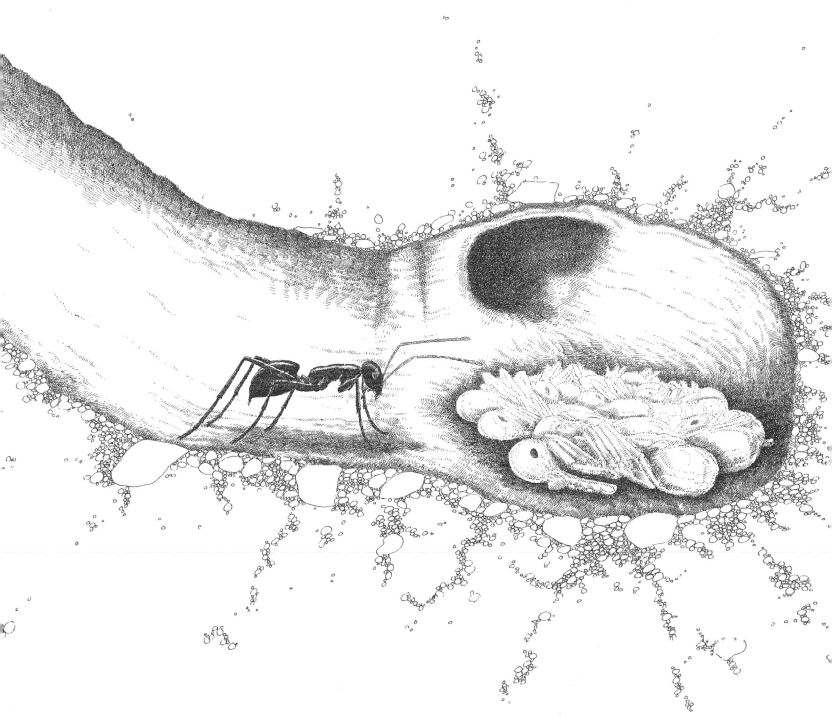

Other scientists are looking at different ways to control the ants. Researchers are looking for ways to disrupt the ants' odor signals. For example, a constant alarm odor might cause the fire-ant colony to destroy itself. But this kind of control could take many years to develop.

Meanwhile, the fire ant continues to multiply and spread throughout the southern United States. We will probably never be able to get rid of the fire ant completely. It looks as if we will just have to keep down their numbers the best way we can and learn to live with the "unconquered" ant.

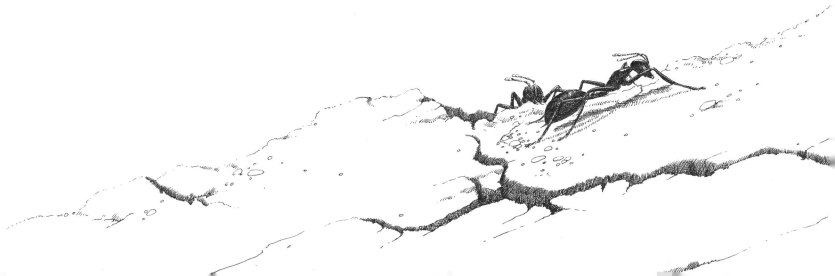

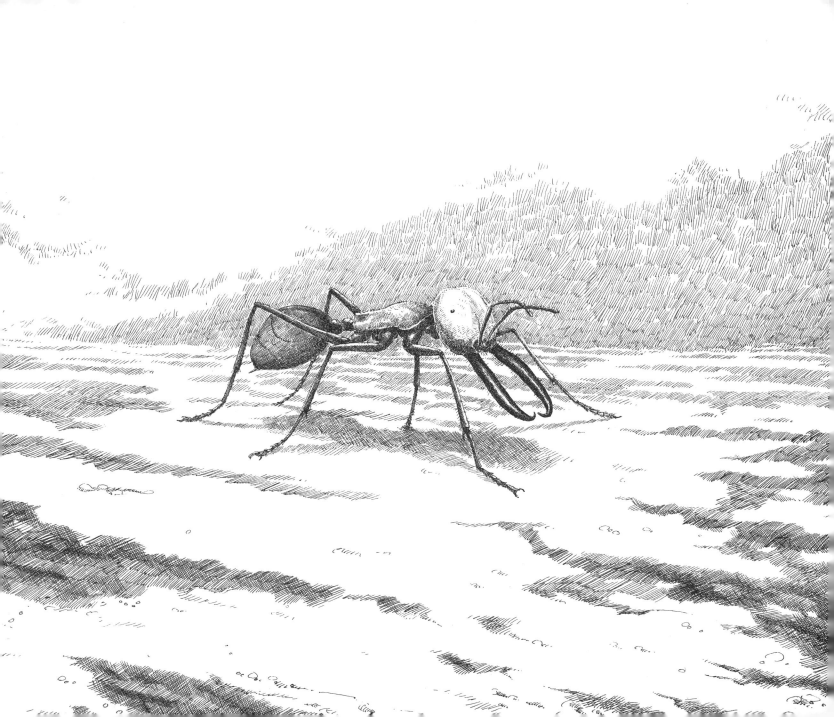

ARMY ANTS

There are about two hundred and fifty different kinds of army ants. They make up a subfamily of ants known as *Dorylinae*. The name comes from a Greek word meaning spear.

Army ants that live in Africa, Asia, and Australia are sometimes called driver ants. The army ants that live in South and Central America are sometimes called legionary ants.

Army ants live in very large colonies. Even the smallest colonies of army ants consist of at least one hundred thousand individuals. Other kinds have colonies that approach one million. And some kinds have colonies that contain over *twenty million ants*. That is more ants in one colony than there are people in New York City, Chicago, and Los Angeles combined.

Most colonies of army ants have a single queen. The queen is the largest ant in the colony. She is wingless and usually totally blind.

The workers in an army-ant colony are of different sizes from very tiny to very large. Small workers spend most of their time in the nest caring for the queen and the young.

Medium-sized workers go out on raids as well as doing other jobs.

The largest workers are over one-half inch long. They have huge heads and powerful jaws. These are the soldiers. They carry back no food on raids but run along on the outside of the raiding parties as a kind of attacking force.

When a soldier meets an enemy, it rears up on its back legs. Its jaws open and close rapidly. The tips of the jaws are very sharp and are curved. A small insect can be cut in two by a snap of the jaws. If a soldier bites a person, its jaws break through the skin and hang on tightly.

An army-ant colony may also have a small number of males. The males are large and winged and look like wasps. Unlike the blind queens and workers, the males have good eyesight. The queen, the workers, and the males are often so different that they don't look as if they belong to the same colony.

Army ants feed on animal foods. They go out on huge raids in which most of the colony takes part. Unlike many other kinds of ants, an army ant never looks for food by itself. All raiding is carried out by great groups of ants moving closely together.

Army ants march in such huge numbers that any animal that doesn't run away will be eaten. This includes small animals from cockroaches to mice. But larger animals such as boa constrictors, monkeys, and even humans have to avoid an army-ant raiding party.

Houses are sometimes invaded by a swarm of army ants and the human inhabitants are forced to leave for a while. But when the humans return, they find the house cleaned out of cockroaches, spiders, and other such pests.

A classic short story about army ants is titled "Leiningen Versus the Ants." The author, Carl Stephenson, sets his story in the Amazon River Valley of Brazil. Leiningen is a plantation owner whose lands become surrounded by an unbelievably large mass of army ants.

Leiningen defends his farmland behind rivers of rapidly flowing water and ditches filled with burning gasoline. At one point the author describes hordes of army ants as a black mass stretching for miles around in every direction. Leiningen finally saves the plantation by running through hundreds of yards of ant columns to open the gates of a dam, flooding the land and stopping the ants.

The story is dramatic and interesting, but there is very little truth in it. The number of army ants described is many more than would really be in even the largest raiding parties. Also, the army ants in the story seem to act as intelligently as would an army of humans. That certainly is not true.

Of course, there are many real stories of army-ant attacks on humans. The famous missionary who explored much of Africa, Dr. David Livingstone, wrote of an escape he made

from army ants. It seems Livingstone was asleep in his tent when he suddenly awoke and saw ants swarming all around. Soon hundreds of biting ants covered his body. Livingstone rushed outside. His men picked the ants off one by one and got him to bed. He was sick for days after his escape.

In truth, almost anyone not asleep could walk more quickly than an advancing column of army ants. But it is certainly possible that a young child left alone, or an elderly or crippled person may not be able to flee fast enough. It is easy to imagine how such a person could be overrun and killed by hundreds of thousands of biting army ants.

There are many stories of people who are bitten by army ants and yet manage to escape. The bite of a single army ant is painful but probably not as bothersome as the sting of a single fire ant. Still, the thought of being bitten is enough to keep most people far away from a raiding party of army ants.

Army-ant raids move out in one of two ways, depending upon the kind of ant. In one kind of raid all the ants move out in a swarm. In the other kind of raid the ants move out in columns. In both kinds of raids the ants behave pretty much the same.

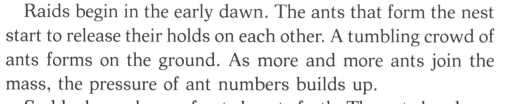

Raids begin in the early dawn. The ants that form the nest start to release their holds on each other. A tumbling crowd of ants forms on the ground. As more and more ants join the mass, the pressure of ant numbers builds up.

Suddenly a column of ants bursts forth. The ants lay down a scent trail as they move. Other ants begin to follow the trail the first ants have left.

The ants at the head of the column hardly seem to be brave leaders. They never move more than a few inches out in front. Even this forward march is caused by all the pushing going on behind them. After being pushed ahead, the leading ants quickly return to the sides of the column.

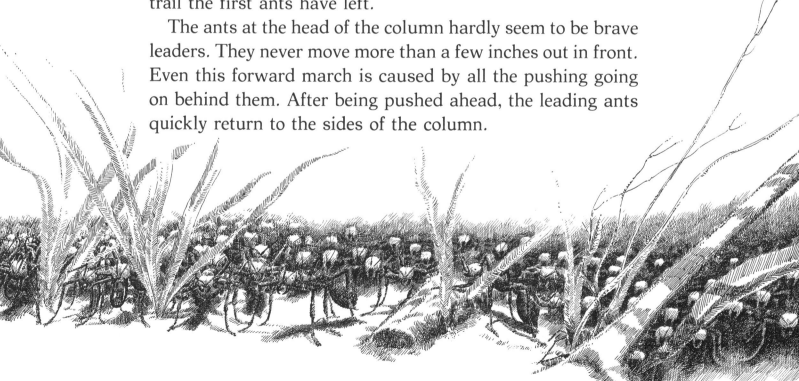

With the leading ants hanging back and the rear ants pushing ahead, the column finally forms a broad swarm. The swarm spreads out as it moves forward. A large raiding swarm may be sixty-five feet across and four to six feet deep.

The pressure of moving ants causes first one part of the swarm to break forward, then another. This results in a kind of encircling movement. In this way, small animals are caught and trapped by the wall of advancing ants. The ants grab any living thing which cannot manage to get away, and bring the soft pieces back to the nest.

The approach of a raiding swarm of army ants can be heard from quite a distance. There is a steady rattling and rustling of plants and leaves as the ants move along and small animals try to escape. Jumping insects knock against tree trunks and branches. Flies buzz around the advancing column. The noise is continuous.

Army-ant raids capture and kill almost any animal life that lies in their path. Their normal prey includes tarantulas, scorpions, spiders, beetles, other kinds of ants, and insects of all kinds. Snakes, lizards, small rodents, and nesting birds are also taken regularly.

African army ants with their sharper jaws and larger colonies capture even larger animals. Goats, dogs, and other domestic animals that are tied or penned up are killed by the encircling swarm of biting ants.

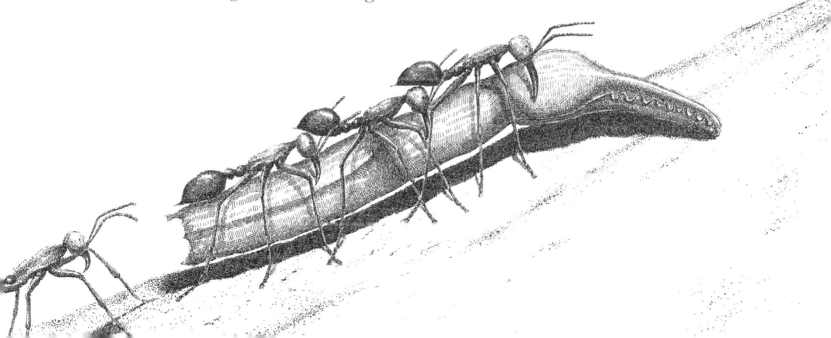

Army ants are true wanderers. They have no fixed home. Their nest is made up of a huge ball of ants hooked one to another. The queen and the young are enclosed deep within the passageways and chambers of the ant mass.

An army-ant colony goes through a five- or six-week cycle of activities. During the first week, the queen's body swells with eggs. At the end of the week she begins to lay thousands of eggs a day. In the second week, the queen may lay as many as one hundred thousand eggs. Only a few of the workers will go out on raids for food. Most workers stay home tending the developing young.

For another ten days the colony will remain in its nest under an overhanging rock or within a hollow tree. The newly laid eggs develop quickly and change into a form called larvae. The larvae look like tiny white caterpillars.

An earlier crop of young ants starts to come out of cocoons called pupae. More raiding parties depart from the nest each day as the new workers join the columns.

One day there is a huge raid, and that evening the nest breaks up and is on the march. The ants swarm out in an enormous mass. Each ant holds to its place in line, following the scent trails of the ants marching ahead. Their antennae move constantly up and down pointing the way to follow.

The column may stretch out for a thousand feet in an unbroken stream. At the rear of the column come the workers carrying the larvae slung beneath them. At the very end the big, wingless queen marches along surrounded and covered by an excited crowd of workers.

For the next two or three weeks the colony wanders, raiding by day and marching in the early evening. Each night the workers hook their bodies together in a temporary nest under a low branch or bush. The next evening the colony breaks up and moves together to a new spot.

Finally the queen begins to swell with eggs again, and the wandering stage is over. The colony settles down and the cycle begins again.

Most kinds of ants live in tropical places, but some are at home in more temperate regions. A few kinds are even found in southern and mid-central United States. The army ants that live in temperate climates have small colonies. They go out on raids, but their foods are mainly other ants and beetles. They may bite if you stumble into a raiding party, but they offer little danger to larger animals or humans.

OTHER DEADLY ANTS

In Africa, Mexico, and Central America grow spiny kinds of trees called acacias. Large numbers of fat, sharp thorns grow all over the branches of these trees. The thorns help protect the trees from being eaten by grazing animals. But acacia trees have another protection as well — ants.

Certain kinds of ants chew their way into the acacias near the sharp tips of the thorns. They set up colonies inside the tree. They also attack any insect that comes to feed on the leaves of the tree. They even chew up any plant that sprouts too near their home tree.

The ants become alert at the smell of an animal or a person. When their tree is shaken, they swarm out in large numbers and attack at once. Their stings are very painful. They cause a long-lasting burning and throbbing. Brushing against an acacia tree is something like walking into a hornet's nest.

Other kinds of ants that you might want to avoid are the bulldog ants of Australia. These are among the largest of all ants. The workers may be one inch long. They look something like wingless wasps.

Bulldog ants move very rapidly over the ground. They have very large eyes and good vision. They also have powerful jaws and a sting which they use on anything or anyone that bothers them.

Bulldog ants will actually chase humans as much as thirty feet away from their nest. Not only do the bulldog ants run quickly, they can even leap several inches when they attack.

The largest ant in the world lives deep in the rain forests of South America. This black ant is called *Dinoponera*, which means "terrible ant." Their long, slender bodies are well over an inch long. These ants have heavy, ragged jaws, and a powerful sting. They live in underground nests containing about one hundred ants.

The natives fear the giant ants because of their stings. One report says that the pain from a sting is very bad for a few minutes, but the numbness can last for a week.

Relatives of these ants are found in many other places around the world. One kind of ant has very large, curved jaws that overlap. When the ant is excited, the jaws open wide. If an insect comes between those jaws it is very likely sliced in two. The ant also has a painful sting which feels much like a bee sting.

There are dozens of ants living in different parts of the world that have painful stings. One of these is a kind of harvester ant that lives in the Arizona desert. There is a legend that the Apache Indians of the Southwest used these ants as a special torture. They tied down an enemy over an ant nest in the desert and left him there to die. That was a painful way indeed to show how deadly some ants can be.